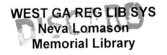

Voting

SARAH DE CAPUA

Children's Press®
An Imprint of Scholastic Inc.
New York   Toronto   London   Auckland   Sydney
Mexico City   New Delhi   Hong Kong
Danbury, Connecticut

Content Consultant
Margaret Heubeck
Youth Leadership Initiative Director of Instruction
University of Virginia Center for Politics
Charlottesville, Virginia

Library of Congress Cataloging-in-Publication Data

De Capua, Sarah
  Voting/by Sarah De Capua.
     p. cm.—(A true book)
  Includes bibliographical references and index.
  ISBN-13: 978-0-531-26043-2 (lib. bdg.) — ISBN-13: 978-0-531-26215-3 (pbk.)
1. Voting—United States—Juvenile literature. 2. Elections—United States—Juvenile literature.
I. Title.
  JK1978.D42 2013
  324.6'50973—dc23   2012000630

All rights reserved. Published in 2013 by Children's Press, an imprint of Scholastic Inc.
Printed in China 62
SCHOLASTIC, CHILDREN'S PRESS, A TRUE BOOK™, and associated logos are trademarks and/or registered trademarks of Scholastic Inc.
1 2 3 4 5 6 7 8 9 10 R 22 21 20 19 18 17 16 15 14 13

Front cover: Vote button
Back cover: Man voting in a booth

Find the Truth!

Everything you are about to read is true *except* for one of the sentences on this page.

Which one is **TRUE**?

T or F   Voting laws are the same in every state in the United States.

T or F   Voters in the United States do not vote directly for the president.

Find the answers in this book.

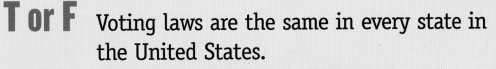

Contents

THE **BIG** TRUTH!

CHAPTER 1

Casting a Vote

Have you ever chosen a leader for your classroom, sports team, Scout pack, or youth group? If the answer is yes, you probably voted. Voting is a way for groups of people to make decisions. It gives each person in the group a voice in choosing leaders and deciding on rules for the group to follow.

The secret ballot was first used in Rome around 1 CE.

Voting: A Hard-Won Right and an Important Responsibility

The U.S. Constitution is a document that contains the laws for setting up the U.S. government and running the country. Fully adopted in 1791, the U.S. Constitution states that citizens who are at least 18 years old have the right to vote in local, state, and nationwide elections.

The Founding Fathers of the United States designed the Constitution to give U.S. citizens a voice in the government.

Until the 15th Amendment was passed in 1870, state and local laws often prevented African Americans from voting.

However, not all countries give their citizens the right to vote. As a result, there have been many conflicts over voting rights. Even in the United States, certain groups struggled for many years for the right to vote. These groups wanted to have a voice in how the country was governed. That is why voting is such an important responsibility, and why the United States encourages its citizens to get out and vote.

In some countries, voting is a legal requirement.

Polls provide voters with private booths so that others cannot see who they are voting for.

Elections

An election is the process of choosing someone or deciding something by voting. Whenever an election is held, it's important that it be free and honest. A free election means that voters have a choice of **candidates** to vote for. An honest election means that people are able to vote by secret ballot. This allows people to vote without fear of being punished because of how they voted.

When people think of voting, they often think of voting for leaders. In the United States, leaders are needed for towns, states, and the nation. Local leaders include city council members and mayors. Governors and lieutenant governors are state leaders. National leaders include the president, vice president, and members of Congress.

Sometimes people also vote on issues. For example, they vote on whether their taxes should be raised. Citizens might also vote on whether a highway should be built through their town. New bills regarding health care, education, and other state and local laws can be voted on as well. Groups sometimes organize a petition, or formal request, to have a certain issue be voted on by the general public.

New residents of the
United States must
become citizens before
they are allowed to vote.

Meeting the Requirements

Each country has its own laws about voting. Here is the way voting works in the United States.

A person must be 18 to vote. Voters must also be American-born or **naturalized** citizens of the United States. Naturalized citizens are people who move to the United States from other countries and then become U.S. citizens.

 Naturalized citizens cannot run for president.

In the months leading up to major elections, volunteers often set up voter registration booths to encourage people to register.

Before Voting

Each state sets its own rules for participating in elections. It is important that voters check their state's voting laws. In most states, citizens have to register before voting. They must fill out registration forms to provide information such as their name, address, and age. They must also show proof of address. A bill, bank statement, or pay stub with their address proves that their address is real.

In some places, people must align themselves with a political party. The United States has two major political parties: the Republican Party and the Democratic Party. A voter who doesn't want to support either of these parties can register as an **independent**. An independent might follow a third party, such as the Libertarian Party or the Green Party.

Barack Obama (D)   John McCain (R)

During presidential elections, the Republican and Democratic parties each choose one nominee.

Voter registration information is kept in an office called the **registrar**. The office is generally located in the voter's city hall or town hall. The registrar keeps a list of all eligible voters living in the area. Usually, a voter's name must show up on the registrar's list before that person can vote.

Citizens can register to vote directly at the registrar's office.

Why Have Parties?

Political parties are important to a republic such as the United States. Basically, political parties provide a way for people with similar interests and goals to band together for political action. Political parties select candidates to run for public office, raise the funds for candidates to campaign, and help inform voters about them. Political parties also explain issues important to an election. When candidates are elected, political parties help them accomplish goals while in office through advice and party support.

Political parties often hold rallies to support their candidates.

The freedom of the press has been guaranteed in the United States since 1791.

Newspapers help citizens learn about important issues during elections.

Staying Informed

Another key step must be taken before a person casts a vote. Responsible voters need to know what they think about important issues. Local races usually focus on issues that matter to the community, such as taxes, building codes, and education. In national races, the focus is on issues that are important to the entire country, such as employment, terrorism, and **immigration**. Sometimes issues in local and national races are the same.

When voting for leaders, voters have a responsibility to learn all they can about the candidates. Candidates are the men and women who are running for office in an election. Candidates give speeches and meet with voters before elections. They explain where they stand on issues that voters care about.

Many candidates meet with voters face-to-face whenever they can.

Getting the Word Out

In elections for major offices such as governor or president, candidates may debate online or on TV. Candidates discuss their ideas for addressing the concerns of voters. Candidates may also have TV, radio, and newspaper ads. Web sites contain information and videos about their positions on certain issues. Citizens may display posters, bumper stickers, and signs to show other voters which candidates they support.

Debates are a great way to learn the differences between candidates.

There are more than 40 political parties in the United States.

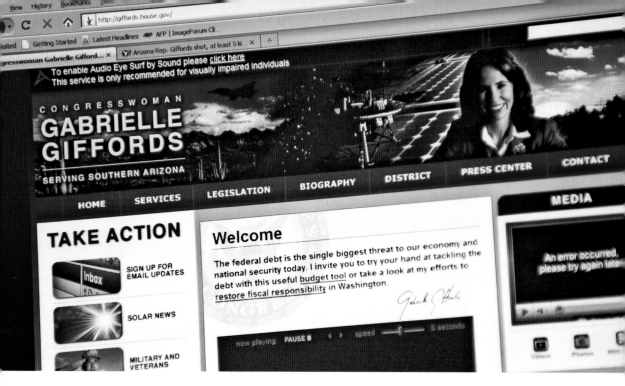

The Internet allows candidates to develop relationships with voters around the country.

Many candidates use social media sites to spread their messages. They set up Facebook pages and Twitter accounts that people can follow. Some candidates create their own YouTube channels, where they post short videos. These videos show them making campaign speeches, volunteering in the community, and talking directly to voters about important issues.

Getting the Vote

When the U.S. Constitution came into effect in 1788, only white men who owned land were allowed to vote. Black Americans, women, Native Americans, and the poor were not eligible to vote. However, over the next 200 years, each of these groups worked hard to gain the right to vote and succeeded.

African American men first legally voted in 1867. Three years later, the 15th Amendment was adopted to guarantee their right to vote. It took nearly 100 years more for that right to become fully protected under the Voting Rights Act of 1965.

Women were granted the right to vote in 1920 through the 19th Amendment. The issue was originally brought to Congress in 1878, but was rejected. It took more than 40 years of organizing and earning the vote in several states for an amendment to be added to the U.S. Constitution.

Before 1924, most Native Americans were not considered U.S. citizens. As a result, they were not allowed to vote. The Indian Citizenship Act of 1924 granted citizenship to all Native Americans born in the United States. This allowed them to legally vote.

Many kinds of buildings serve as polling places on Election Day.

CHAPTER 3

Election Day!

Voters wait for the big day to arrive—Election Day! Election Day is the day set aside by local, state, or national law to hold an election. Presidential elections occur every four years on the first Tuesday following the first Monday of November. Local elections, which concern a much smaller population than presidential elections, may occur in different months or years. Registered voters visit their local polling places on Election Day. Public schools, libraries, churches, and other buildings are often used as polling places.

← Election Day always falls between November 2 and 8.

At the Polling Place

Requirements for checking in at the polling place differ from state to state. Voters can find the requirements by contacting their state's board of elections. After arriving at the polling place, a voter waits in line to see a clerk. She might have to show **identification**, such as a driver's license, to prove who she is. The clerk checks off the voter's name on the registration list. This ensures that each voter casts only one vote.

Voters sometimes have to sign a poll book or other document to check in.

Long-Distance Voting

Sometimes people are not able to vote in person at their assigned polling place on Election Day. Their reasons may include travel, illness, or injury. In these cases, a voter can ask his registrar for an **absentee ballot**. A paper ballot arrives by U.S. mail. The voter completes the ballot and mails it back to his registrar's office. Absentee ballots contain the same list of candidates and issues as the ballots used at the polling place.

CALIFORNIA PRESIDENTIAL
PRIMARY ELECTION
TUESDAY, FEBRUARY 5, 2008

OFFICIAL BALLOT

304900

NONPARTISAN
ALAMEDA COUNTY, CALIFORNIA
FEBRUARY 5, 2008 PRESIDENTIAL PRIMARY ELECTION

INSTRUCTIONS TO VOTERS: USE BLACK OR BLUE BALLPOINT PEN ONLY

To vote for a candidate of your choice, complete the arrow to the right of the candidate's name. To vote for a qualified write-in candidate, PRINT the person's name in the blank space provided and COMPLETE the arrow.
To vote on any measure, complete the arrow after the word "Yes" or "No."

YES
NO

MEASURES SUBMITTED TO THE VOTERS

STATE

PROPOSITION 93: LIMITS ON LEGISLATORS' TERMS IN OFFICE. INITIATIVE CONSTITUTIONAL AMENDMENT. Reduces permissible state legislative service to 12 years. Allows 12

PROPOSITION 97: REFERENDUM ON AMENDMENT TO INDIAN GAMING COMPACT. "Yes" Vote approves, and "No" Vote rejects, a law that ratifies an amendment to existing gaming compact

Special computers are used to scan Marksense ballots.

Casting the Vote

Different polling places use different voting methods. Some use Marksense ballots. Voters use a black marker to color in an empty oval, circle, or rectangle next to an issue or a candidate's name. When they are finished voting, they feed the ballot into a computer. The computer records the dark marks on the ballots as votes.

Many towns use direct recording electronic (DRE) voting systems. A voter receives a pass card from the clerk to insert into a computer. The touch screen lists an issue or the candidates for an office. The voter touches Yes or No for an issue, or the name of the candidate. When the voter presses End, the computer records the votes and the pass card pops out. Then the voter returns the pass card to the clerk.

DRE machines use touch screens to record votes.

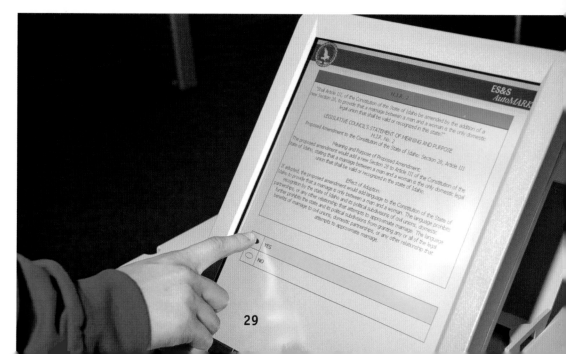

Some polling places use punch card ballots. Voters are given a ballot card, which they clip onto a metal device. They use the device's **stylus** to poke holes to indicate the candidates or issues they support. After voting, they feed their ballot into a computer. The computer reads the punched holes and records the votes.

Punch card voting requires the use of special machines.

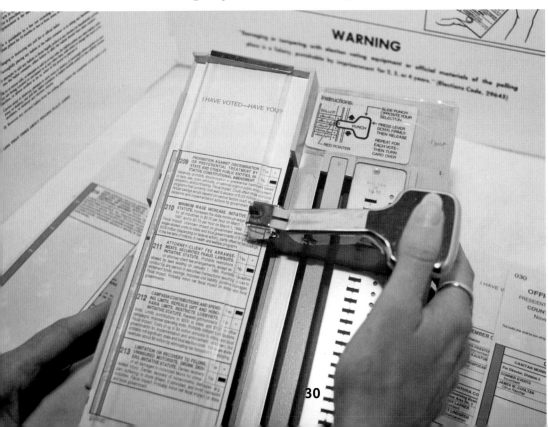

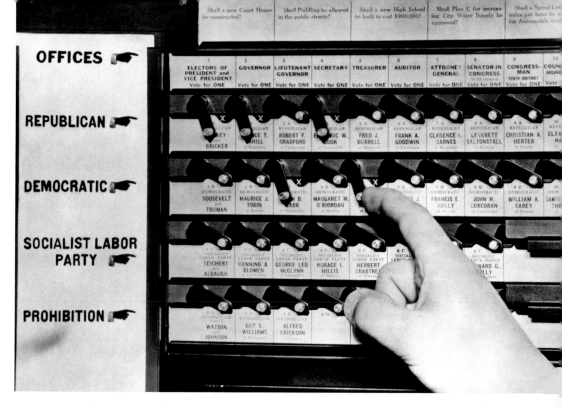

Lever machines were invented in the 1890s.

Lever machines are another method of voting. A voter steps up to the machine and pulls a large lever that closes a privacy curtain. To cast a vote, the voter pulls down small levers located above the candidates' names. When there are issues on the ballot, the voter pulls the lever for Yes or No. When the voter pulls the large lever again to open the curtain, the votes are recorded inside the machine.

In some places, paper ballots are used. Voters simply write an X next to the names of their chosen candidates. They place an X beside Yes or No when they are voting on issues.

In all of these voting methods, privacy is very important. Booths, curtains, and **partitions** are used to ensure that voters can mark their ballots in secret.

Most voters do not want other people to see whom they vote for.

Each state determines the hours for voting. Some polling places are open from 6 a.m. until 8 or 9 p.m. This ensures that everyone can find a time to vote, even if they have busy schedules. In some elections, there is heavy turnout with many people waiting in line to vote. When this happens, special permission may be given to keep polling places open later so everyone has a chance to vote.

Lines often form at polling places during the busiest parts of the day.

Volunteers carefully count each ballot after the polls close.

CHAPTER 4

Keeping Count

Counting the votes correctly is an important part of any election. When the polls close, volunteers at each polling place collect the vote totals. Polling places that used computerized ballots generally have totals that are produced automatically. If paper ballots were used, the volunteers count each one by hand.

 The first U.S. presidential election took place between 1788 and 1789.

Announcing the Winners

Depending on how many votes must be counted, it can take several hours to determine the winner. When clerks at each polling place have finished counting the votes, the results are announced to the public. People learn the results through television, Internet, newspapers, and radios. Voters who follow their favorite candidates on Facebook or Twitter can also watch those sites for the announcement.

News programs and Web sites devote several hours on Election Night to announcing the results of nationwide elections.

In the presidential election of 2000, it took 36 days to find out who won!

Candidates often hold rallies on election night as they wait for the election results.

National elections occur on the same day all across the United States. Presidential elections are national elections that involve voting for the president and vice president. Congressional elections are local, or sometimes statewide, elections for members of Congress. In these elections, millions of votes must be counted. Sometimes it is very late at night—or early the next morning—before the public knows who won.

The Electoral College

Presidential elections are different from other elections in the way the winner is determined. In the United States, citizens do not vote directly for the president. The vote that is cast actually goes to an **elector** who is pledged to a certain candidate. Electors gather together and form the Electoral College. Each state has a certain number of electors, based on its population. The larger a state's population, the more electors it gets. Some states have as few as three electors, while others have as many as 55.

Timeline of U.S. Voting History

1787

The U.S. Constitution is signed.

1870

The 15th Amendment grants African American men the right to vote.

1920

The 19th Amendment grants women the right to vote.

In some states, the candidate who wins the popular vote gets all of the state's electoral votes. The exceptions are Maine and Nebraska, which can split their electoral votes. During a presidential race, the electors do not cast their actual votes until after the popular election, when the Electoral College meets. There are 538 total electoral votes available, and a presidential candidate needs to win more than half of them to win the election.

1924
The Indian Citizenship Act grants U.S.-born Native Americans U.S. citizenship, and thus the right to vote.

2008
More than 130 million people vote in the U.S. presidential election.

for
PRESIDENT

BALLOTS

Schools often hold
election for student
government positions.

SMITH
for

CHAPTER 5

Getting Involved

Even though you can't vote in local, state, or national elections until you're 18, you can be involved in politics right now. Become active in classroom or school elections. Accompany an adult to the polls. You can discuss the candidates and issues in upcoming elections. Do you have opinions about the candidates? Which issues do they support? What kinds of campaign promises do they make?

Before 1971, the legal voting age was 21.

Get to Know Your Government

Ask an adult to help you learn more about the elected officials in your community. You can write e-mails or letters to these officials. Tell them what you think they should do about issues that concern you. You might also be able to convince the candidate to visit your school.

Politicians often visit schools to help educate students about important issues.

Even if you are too young to vote, you can help support your favorite candidate in other ways.

When a candidate you like is running for office, volunteer to help adults put up posters and yard signs around your community. You can help out at campaign headquarters, too. Dedicated helpers are always needed to help with basic office tasks. You might find yourself getting caught up in the excitement of the campaign. Someday, you might even run for office yourself! ★

Number of people in the United States who voted in the 2008 election: More than 130 million

State with the highest number of electors: California (55)

States with the lowest number of electors: Alaska, Delaware, Montana, North Dakota, South Dakota, Vermont, Wyoming (3 each)

First people to choose their leaders by voting: Ancient Greeks, who lived more than 2,500 years ago

First people to vote by secret ballot: Ancient Romans, about 2,000 years ago

The only state where people do not have to register to vote: North Dakota

State where the most U.S. presidents were born: Virginia

The youngest person ever to serve as president: Theodore Roosevelt, age 42 (1901)

The oldest person ever elected president: Ronald Reagan, age 69 (1980)

Did you find the truth?

F Voting laws are the same in every state in the United States.

T Voters in the United States do not vote directly for the president.

Resources

Books

Cheney, Lynne. *We the People: The Story of Our Constitution*. New York: Simon & Schuster Children's Publishing, 2008.

Christelow, Eileen. *Vote!* New York: Clarion Books, 2008.

Lishak, Antony. *Elections and Voting*. North Mankato, MN: Smart Apple Media, 2008.

Steele, Philip. *Vote*. New York: DK Publishing, 2008.

Visit this Scholastic Web site for more information on voting:

★ www.factsfornow.scholastic.com
Enter the keyword **Voting**

Important Words

absentee ballot (ab-suhn-TEE BAL-uht) — a voting form filled out and sent in by a voter who could not be present at his or her polling station on Election Day

candidates (KAN-di-dates) — people who are running in an election

elector (i-LEK-tor) — a member of the U.S. Electoral College who casts a vote for the president

identification (eye-den-tuh-fi-KAY-shuhn) — a document or other item that proves who a person is

immigration (im-i-GRAY-shuhn) — the movement of a person from one country to live permanently in another

independent (in-di-PEN-duhnt) — a citizen who does not identify with Republicans or Democrats

naturalized (NACH-ur-uh-lized) — made a citizen of a country where one was not born

partitions (par-TISH-uhnz) — movable walls or panels used to divide an area or a room

registrar (REJ-is-trar) — an official keeper of records

stylus (STYE-luhs) — a small stick used like a pen to input data to some devices

Index

Page numbers in **bold** indicate illustrations

About the Author

Sarah De Capua is the author of many nonfiction titles for children. She enjoys helping young readers learn about our country through civics education. When it comes to voting, she would like them to experience the same excitement she felt as a child the first time her mother took her into a voting booth to show her how to vote. De Capua works as a children's book author and editor, as well as a college composition instructor. She holds a master's degree in teaching from Sacred Heart University in Connecticut, and is currently working toward her doctorate in composition and TESOL at Indiana University of Pennsylvania. She has written other True Books in this set, including *Paying Taxes*, *Serving on a Jury*, and *Running for Public Office*.

PHOTOGRAPHS © 2013: age fotostock/Spencer Grant: back cover; Alamy Images: 3, 10, 29, 39 right (David R. Frazier Photolibrary, Inc.), 24 (Doug Schneider), 32 (Frances Roberts), 12 (Jeff Greenberg), 26, 43 (Jim West), 5 bottom, 27, 44 (Rene Paik), 6 (TongRo Images), 15 (ZUMA Wire Service); AP Images: 34 (Elaine Thompson), 28 (Mike Groll), 33 (Mike Knaak/St. Cloud Times), 16 (Steve Helber), 5 top, 17 (Sue Kroll/NBC NewsWire); Corbis Images/Junius Brutus Stearns/Bettmann: 8, 38 left; Getty Images: 20 (Joe Raedle), 37 (Mark Wilson/Newsmakers), 21 (Nicholas Kamm/AFP), 4, 36 (Virginia Sherwood/NBC/NBCU Photo Bank); iStockphoto/spxChrome: cover; Landov/Brian Snyder/Reuters: 42; Library of Congress/National Photo Company: 23 bottom, 39 left; Media Bakery: 18 (Christopher Robbins), 40; Shutterstock, Inc./Vince Clements: 22, 23 background; Superstock, Inc.: 23 center, 38 right (Everett Collection), 30 (Visions of America), 31; The Granger Collection: 9, 23 top; The Image Works: 19 (Marilyn Humphries), 14 (Marjorie Kamys Cotera/Daemmrich Photography).